Bonsai Tree Care Bailout – A Beginner's Bonsai Guide

For More Free Videos And Expert Tips on
Growing Amazing Bonsai go to
http://BonsaiUnderground.com

For more information about bonsai
from this author check out the book our other books
on Amazon here
www.amazon.com/author/littlepearl

Foreword

Being asked to write a foreword of this kind is a weird and irresistible honor, and the premise sounded solid — give 'em something they can get started with that is neither Kung foolishness/woo-woo, nor some high handed drivel that this art form attracts like offal flies..... So, let us begin in that spirit, and Devil take the hindmost, as always.

All those who yearn to make a buck from their hobby must invariably claim close friendship with the late John Naka to achieve a patina of respectability: so be it. Here is the Naka quote you can take to the bank. When asked how to make good bonsai, he always answered "Begin with good material". The rest is filigree....

But I have to write something, so here begins a list of do's and dont's: 1) Learn how to find and recognize good material, and don't waste uber-precious time on crap. Fewer-and-better is always preferable to more-and-feeble. 2) Get the best tools you can comfortably afford, but don't mortgage the farm. The whole tool thing becomes a fetish, and it's crazy to work on fifty cent plants with two hundred dollar shears. 3) Choose plants that do well in your climate, and use natives when possible. You'd have to be an imbecile to nurse Japanese Maples along in a place like Socorro, New Mexico (oops!). 4) Learn what's best for you to do where you are (soils, fertilizers, etc.), and not what's best for some crypto-sensei who lives in a totally different climate. 5) If all else fails, move to Oregon with Roger C. — tell him I sent you, and you'll be greeted appropriately! 6) For God's sake, approach the art and your material with humility and a beginner's mind. 7) Find a good teacher, if you can, who can show you a way to proceed that, left to your own insecurity and self-obsession, you would not otherwise see......

Oh, oh.... slipping into woo-woo city there a bit, but you should acquaint yourself with the Zen underpinnings of bonsai. Your continuing study should be accompanied by the loud squeaking sound of your head being pulled from your own rear end....

Right! and here's what I'd say NOT to do: 1) Do not fall into the pathetic status consciousness thing that Bonsai politics breeds like rats. Tend your own garden, do your work, find your zone. 2) Do not, however, let your manifest authority problem result in an "I'll do it my damn way!" mentality. Your way is dog dung, as it is for all beginners. There are no bonsai prodigies. Everybody is a moron for about two years — don't make that period any longer. 3) Related to #1, beware of those whose main bonsai skill is self-promotion. Any lint-head who calls him/herself a "master" is not, by definition. A fine old Zen saying applies: "If you meet the Buddha in the road, kill him!". 4) Don't rush to commit seppuku whenever a plant dies (or "goes to live somewhere else" as MY DEAR FRIEND (ho, ho!) Mr. Naka used to say). Often, a higher pay grade than you is in charge of such things. Do your best.

Good God! Speaking of high-handed! But please folks.... remember that we're working on a tragically stupid deadline pressure here. Knowest thou that I could do better with adequate time, don't you?..... DON'T YOU???

Get into the dirt and get your hands and face filthy and stinking of liquid fish! Go to the zone with your little green friends and don't come back for hours! Let Bonsai change your view of reality.... and YOU, JOSHUA! hold that ludicrous deadline two more minutes!!

John Egert
Socorro, New Mexico
March 3, 2012

Miyagi: Wax on... wax off. Wax on... wax off.
Daniel: When do I learn how to punch?
Miyagi: Better learn balance. Balance is key. Balance good,
          karate good. Everything good. Balance bad, better
          pack up, go home. Understand?

Attention Arboreal Nymphs!!!

It is time, once again, for the Biomassacre at your local bonsai club (check local listings). But before we go further, we must come to grips with the firestorm of mutinous lunacy that nearly caused my last month's class to end in a muddle of rage and recriminations.

We will be meeting in the coming chapters, so get ready. Read this book inside and out, then easily create a fine Bonsai collection almost overnight; train 99 bonsai trees and keep one (maybe two or three maximum).

And remember, the fusion of Japanese gardens and great bonsai is mere simplicity.

What else? Any other vital matters I am forgetting? Oh yes...SARU NO AKAI SHIRI O WARAUNA. Translation, "Don't laugh at the other monkey's red butt."

— **Master Joshua Rothman**

More information can be found by heading over to http://www.bonsaiunderground.com for free videos and information

Table of Contents

Welcome Tree Toads!

For you skeptics out there wondering why in the world you should listen to me, Joshua Rothman, here is one of the best reasons I have. My sensei has now been practicing the art of bonsai nearly forty years, and his original teacher was the world renown, John Naka, American Bonsai Master.

"A bonsai can never be a finished work of art...because it will always be a living piece of nature, continuing to live and grow. The object is not to make the tree look like a bonsai, but to make the bonsai look like a tree."

— **John Naka**

A Brief History

Miyagi: [drunk] Banzai!
Daniel: [totally confused] To baby trees.
Miyagi: Not bonsai, BANZAI!

The term bonsai (literally 'tree in a pot') is of Japanese origin and refers to a specific type of art form that grew out of Japanese culture and has been transplanted in various forms around the world. Bonsai though, as we know it today, came from China.

The art of Penjing, cultivating plants in pots, has been traced by some scholars as far back as 500 BC, but we know from paintings that plants artistically designed in pots were being cultivated from at least 600 AD in China. During the Tang Dynasty (618-907 AD), this art form was greatly influenced by the landscape painting and garden art that was flourishing at the time. It is believed that the art of Penjing was carried to Japan, Korea, and other Asian countries by wandering Buddhist monks. In fact, bonsai and Buddhism are deeply intertwined, particularly in Japan.

Once bonsai had established itself in Japan, it developed a distinctive aesthetic derived from Japanese culture, and underwent generations of refinement. It also developed different schools and styles. There are, though, basic bonsai principals that, having been passed down from bonsai masters to students for generations, deeply influence the art. And, only by mastering these principals and techniques, can the bonsai artist free himself creatively to explore new directions for the art form to take.

Bonsai Philosophy and Wisdom

PHILOSOPHY

You're balancing strength and grace all the time.

Everyone one of us has to make up our mind which route we're going with depending on the tree material. Always DO more with less. Symmetry is BAD; balance is good.

Sometimes, that's hard for western minds to grasp. Asymmetrical balance is key, and for many westerners this can become a huge stumbling block. You're trying to reduce your specimen to less, with the minimal amount of branches that will get the job done.

Ultimately, you want a *dream* of a tree, not a perfect miniature tree. Instead bonsai should be nothing but a suggestion that transports you into the world of that tree.

Yes, there is a lot of thinking to this art, but it very quickly becomes second nature. It's like music – you're playing your stupid little "Twinkle Twinkle Little Star", wondering when you're ever going to learn how to play the real songs, and then one day you can all of a sudden play classical masterpieces. All of a sudden, in that moment, you get almost a second sense.

Yes, there is a lot of thinking to this art, but it very quickly becomes second nature. It's like music - you're playing your stupid little "Twinkle Twinkle Little Star", wondering when you're ever going to learn how to play the real songs, and then one day you can all of a sudden play classical masterpieces. All of a sudden, in that moment, you get almost a second sense.

If you take off for a year, your mind can pick it right back up again.
The frame of reference is always there, in an old tree in nature that
has endured and survived.

"For 26 years I've been doing bonsai. After hiking in the surroundings of my native southwest, my bonsai begin to look more like the natural material around me. You begin to notice that you create what you see. Even though we're on the same parallel as Japan... does this (my tree) look like Japan to you? In your thinking process with bonsai, create what you see. This is the key. "

— **American Bonsai Master In New Mexico**

"Do not seek to follow in the footsteps of the masters; seek what they sought."

— **Famous Zen Saying**

THE WISDOM AND ORIGIN OF BONSAI

Bonsai is an Asian tradition tracing back roots for centuries as an artistic, symbolic recreation of nature. Bonsai is an abstraction of nature that combines the aesthetics of fine art with the skills or horticulture.

To the vast many, bonsai may seem like merely the growing of dwarfed trees and horrendous torturing through small pots and wire. However rather than producing an exact replica, the true bonsai artist uses nature as his canvas to develop and evoke a strong natural sense. The bonsai becomes the focal point of the painting and the artist creates a sense of mood and setting by sculpting it to create an even deeper sense of wonder that invites the viewer into the aura of the miniature delight.

A bonsai develops from a combination of what you feel about the tree and how the tree behaves. There is no actual conflict between the natural element of chance and the human element of control, but there is a constant compromise.

It is the plant - the roots and trunk, the branches, the twigs and the leaves - as much the trunk and branches that determine how a bonsai will develop. Too many new students feel that they have created a bonsai, and often it will be years before they realize that their effort is only a small contribution to the plant and the bonsai that results.

Trees have their own personalities and cannot be expected to behave the same as another tree of the same species, or even of the same variety. Every pine does not behave like every other pine; every black pine cannot be expected to develop the same as another black pine. And, it would be a mistake for you to treat every pine alike.

On the other hand, your feeling about every black pine will not be the same. The development of the plant is a result of what you feel and what nature offers. It is a compromise between nature's random growth and the control you exercise to that growth.

The ultimate goal in shaping a bonsai is an elusive, ethereal thing rather than an inflexible blueprint of future development. It is a changing, growing thing that you guide from year to year with no real completion time or ending point. The enjoyment of bonsai is giving some control to nature's seemingly purposeless growth.

It is important to note that a fine bonsai is regarded by the Japanese as much more than merely a tiny tree grown in a handful of earth. It is a magnified landscape from nature in its purest form; nature's essence is the main focal point. The bonsai artist composes his creation upon the canvas of an untrained raw material tree and expertly trains the trunk and each individual branch to compose natural harmony and character. Simplicity is key.

Today in Japan there are many bonsai known to be several hundred years old that have been passed down from generation to generation, each tree containing an amazing history. This chapter was written to help guide you in your journey, to learn to cultivate bonsai you love, and instruct how to enjoy this unique art form that has been prized and practiced in Japan for centuries.

"You want a dream of a tree. Not a perfect miniature tree. A suggestion that transports you into the world of that tree."

— John (bonsai guru)

"A bonsai truly represents the fusion of nature and human wisdom; it is an art that at once pursues the spirits of both nature and beauty."

— Amy Liang

"The aesthetic sensibilities of bonsai, which have their roots in the Zen tradition, contribute very significantly to the total experience of bonsai, which is about beauty, peace, and tranquility."

— Peter Chan

"Bonsai combines heaven and earth in one container. Bonsai with it's pot and soil is physically independent of the earth since its roots are not actually planted in it. It is a separate entity complete in itself, yet it is a part of nature and the beauty of simplicity."

— Wisdom from a wise bonsai ninja

And, there really should be no final goal for the development of your bonsai, for, if you were to achieve it, there would be nothing to strive for, and for the bonsai student, striving is the goal. There is a proverb that says to travel well is better than to arrive. Patience is a virtue, and a true bonsai does not happen overnight. The journey and process are much more important than the destination; savor it. Go forth! And conquer... create great bonsai!

Ideal Locations For Bonsai Survival

Although you may want to showcase your bonsai on the most prominent table in your house or next to the dinner table for special occasions, listen to this first. Remember that bonsai trees are not like typical houseplants, far from it. Oftentimes, humidity levels indoors and low light levels can quickly deplete the health of the tree and leave it gasping for life. With exception to the winter and harsh freezing temperatures, bonsai should be exposed to the fresh air where they can easily uptake sunlight and thrive.

WARNING: Keep bonsai out of extreme heat, sun, blistering winds and pounding rain or hail at all costs! No pot left behind.

If you do get lazy, your bonsai will get eaten for lunch and tossed to the dogs. At best have a secure covered area or spare room of your house to move trees during extreme weather or storms. Many bonsai experts provide adequate shade and shelter with latticework, bamboo screens or shade cloth from the local hardware store to help filter harsh sunlight.

Individually, some bonsai that are shade lovers will require more shade and those that require more light may need to be moved around to suit the specimen's particular need. Be sure to never overcrowd your trees by leaving at least 12 inches between them. It is a good practice to position them on a raised bed or table to prevent animals and pets from damaging them.

Critical Tools To Bailout Your Bonsai

Daniel: *[practicing blocks in Mr. Miyagi's boat] When am I gonna learn how to punch?*

Miyagi: *Learn how punch, after you learn how keep dry! [Rocks boat, throwing Daniel into the water]*

Very well, Tree Toads!!!! Another chapter is bearing down on us all about bonsai tools. And, as always, I am dangerously behind the Kosmic Kurve.

But do not fear, Beloved Ones, we will be ready to eat Siberian Elms and crap 2X4's come Saturday. We should have a selection of our new bonsai enthusiasts, so some time will be spent on what's workin' in terms of tools, wire, and such — I am blatantly sharing all info that might prevent you newbies from buying the $200 tweezers set that you are looking at buying right now.

Onward to tools!

There is a whole industry built around handcrafted bonsai tools. Truthfully, to begin you only need a few critical tools and as you become more skilled in your bonsai techniques you can gradually make the next step.

I often find my bonsai tools for a great price at DallasBonsai.com. (This is not an affiliate link - I would just you rather not spend countless hours surfing the web for overpriced crap. These guys are good!)

BASIC TOOLS TO GET YOUR HANDS DIRTY

1. **Pointed nose shears with a spring to help leverage.**
    Overall, this is a very helpful tool because it has many uses
    in cutting off lots of small branches. Most people will tell
    you not to use this type of shear on root pruning, however, if
    it's all you've got it will work just fine. Just be sure to clean
    your tools.

2. **Pointed nose shears with slip-through looped handle.** This
    tool is especially great for trimming small branches and
    roots.

These **Small trimmer with slim handle and finger control are
nice for smaller branches.** This is essential for trimming twigs, old
flower buds, old berries or for leave cutting. It's a nice tool to have
for those harder to reach places.

3. **Large trimmers.** These are much better for cutting stronger larger branches or roots. These are typically the branch cutter you find at the local hardware store.

4. **KUIKIRI trimmer.** It is specially designed so that it cuts deeper into a branch or root without leaving a knob. The result is a concave cut which is much cleaner and promotes faster healing. This tool can also be used to cut a branch at the base or for cutting most other branches.

5. **Folding saw.** This guy is used to saw a root, branch or truck that cannot be cut with other tools. Having a sharp saw like this is also super useful when hunting bonsai trees in the wild and it is necessary to cut back old deadwood, branches and roots that have collected over the years.

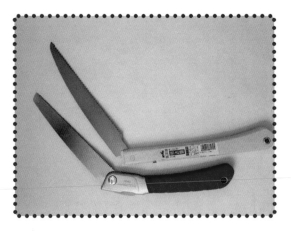

6. **Grafting knife.** A very handy tool in many ways as it provides an extremely sharp blade that becomes useful when grafting, budding, etc.

7. **Wire cutters.** This is used for cutting both large and small bonsai wire in the training process.

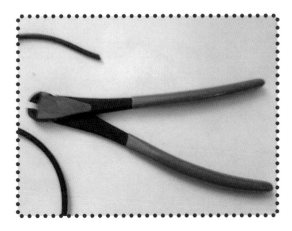

8. **JIN pliers.** JIN pliers are used on branches and trunks to help create natural deadwood effects and for removing bark.

9. **Chopsticks or fiberglass sticks.** This is an essential tool for any bonsai warrior's tool chest. These amazing sticks will not only help you choose the "front" of your bonsai, but they help keep your bonsai "front" in place when you are training a bonsai, allowing you to train the branches around this angle. The chopsticks can also aid in repotting to clear away old soil and untangle the roots, or even to tamp soil in between roots and compact the soil during transplanting.

10. **Claw.** This is used for removing soil and and detangling roots during transplanting.

11. **Sprinkling can with fine nose.** Used for delicate watering, a fine sprinkler attached to your garden hose is also fine.

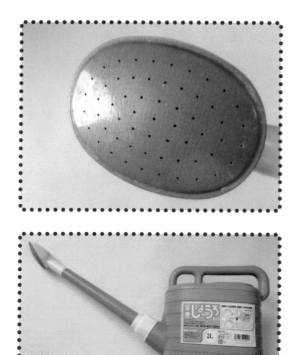

12. **Pick Ax or Hole Digger.** Used for harvesting bonsai from the wild and to uproot stubborn old trees; get a good one, you'll need it.

OTHER GOODIES FOR THE JOURNEY

1. **Tree Seal or Cut Paste:** Things like commercial tree
    seal, pinesap, tree-resin, mud, tape, you get the idea. It's
    important to cover any fresh cuts or wounds on the branches
    or roots of your bonsai to prevent bacteria and pests from
    invading its home.

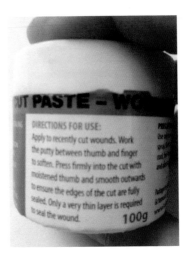

2. **Super-thrive and Vitamin-B1** are your best friends! Use these two in conjunction whenever transplanting or to stimulate a weakened tree to maximize recovery and stabilize the tree's health.

3. **Rooting hormone** for cuttings or drastic transplanting where large areas of roots have been removed. This will help stimulate lush new roots immediately.

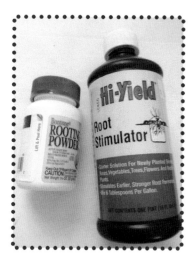

4. **Twine, raffia, cloth, plastic-tape or rubber tube** for protecting the trunk and branch from the wire used for training.

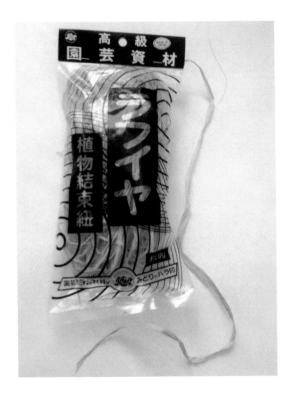

5. **Forget everything** you learned about plants and gardening. Bring a humble attitude. Remember, bonsai is a journey not a destination.

THE "HOW-TO-KEEP-YOUR-TOOLS-SQUEAKY-CLEAN" CHECKLIST

Would you buy a Lexus or Cadillac and never change the oil?
Once you've invested in a few valuable bonsai tools you'll want to increase the lifespan of your tools so that they are ready to go when you need them and so you don't break the bank by wasting all your money. Here are some tips for tools:

1. Clean with alcohol and use a scouring pad to remove sap, soil and other residue.

2. Oil. DW-40 or other chain lubricants will work just fine.

3. WARNING: Do not leave tools outdoors or in a damp place. (The metal will oxidize and your tools will be brown within days.)

4. Keep tools sharpened.

5. Hang your sprinkling can upside down after use to drain water and avoid bacteria problems.

Natural Ideas: Nature Sparks Ideas For Amazing Bonsai. Just Look...

One of the most amazing places on earth to go and be in the presence of God's bonsai trees is the great and glorious Muir Woods outside of San Francisco, California. The magnificent redwoods in Muir Woods are a sample of God's bonsai collection.

Here are some pictures of Muir Woods from this past summer. Nature is the ideal place to get ideas for your bonsai. Real trees age by nature's intricate patterns for which you can model after. The result of this process is a great looking bonsai.

Enjoy these pictures and get some ideas.

Natural Ideas: Nature Sparks Ideas For Amazing Bonsai, Just Look...

31

Natural Ideas: Nature Sparks Ideas For Amazing Bonsai, Just Look...

33

This wine tree in Napa Valley California reflects a nice character with it's twisted old trunk which happens in nature.

Bonsai Selection: A Ninja's Ultimate Approach To Bonsai

Miyagi:	Go, find balance. [chuckles]
Daniel:	[starts to drive away]
Miyagi:	Banzai, Daniel-san.
Daniel:	Hey, banzai!
Miyagi:	[beat; then, louder] Banzai!
Daniel:	[louder] Banzai!
Miyagi:	[shouts] Banzai!
Daniel:	[shouts back] Banzai!

"Give space for the birds and butterflies to fly through the branches when creating your masterpiece"

— **John Naka**

Well, Dear Souls, I hate to say this, but it's time for yet another agonizing reappraisal and hellish introspection. It irritates me that there has been an over manipulation of trees lately. People are getting crazy and using paint and stains on their trees. Let's get back to nature folks. And before any of you chowder-heads roll your bloodshot, cataract-ridden eyes, let me ask how YOUR little trees are enjoying the summer, and how did they like last winter?

It has finally occurred to me, delayed no doubt by the onset of senility and my well-known ingestion of hazmat-style chemicals in a somewhat younger day, that the greatest obstacle to our doing the first-class bonsai is not in choosing dog-meat material, nor any great lack of technique, but rather our preternaturally goofy climate and uncontrollable weather conditions. The reality is that no human activity short of dog sledding is as ill suited to places like the Southwest part of the United States as the art of bonsai. If you live elsewhere, God bless you.

Now, I know that many of you will make a retching sound and whip your index fingers around your immense ears in the classic "fruit-loop" motion, wondering why it took me this long to get the drift. Never mind. We will address these issues on a general approach to bonsai once and for all in an intense and soul-ripping attempt to state the problem definitively, and to offer as many solutions as we can suggest, regarding the ability to keep trees healthy and attractive. The prospects for total failure and psychotic breakdown are very real. You are warned. So, read this and get to work on your little trees!

"In order to grow amazing Bonsai, there are some guidelines to follow and balance as you begin to orchestrate your nature show."

— **Master Jun Ree**

"... The ultimate challenge for the bonsai designer is to expose the essence of the tree."

— **Herb L. Gustafson**

A NINJA'S GUIDELINES

1. **IMPORTANT: Start with great material.** Get this correct and
    you're already ahead of 98% of the people "trying" to create
    or grow bonsai.

    Select hardy plants. Conifers (being pines and junipers)
    are mostly used and representative of bonsai in general.
    Juniper varieties are especially good and tend to grow
    faster and recover quicker than their close relatives in the
    pine family. Also, it is good to note that pine tree varieties,
    although extremely hardy, often present a greater challenge
    for the beginner just getting started because they lack good
    workable branches and grow slower than snails.

2. **Don't overindulge at the tree mart and bring a giant tree home just yet!** It is much more practical to start with a small size, but not too small. A good rule of thumb would be using a 1-gallon size or a 5-gallon size for beginning bonsai trees. From this size pot the finished size will be somewhere around 6 to 10 inches in height after pruning and styling.

3. **5 Golden Rules For Selecting The Perfect Bonsai One...**
Rootage: The root should spread in all directions. These
roots should be divided at the base of the trunk.

Two...Trunk: Take a look down into the pot (you might have to clear away dead materials just to see). At the very least, the trunk should be stocky and tapered as it goes upwards.

Three...Apex: Every tree has an apex, so the same goes for your bonsai. Even after the tip has been cut, a proper branch that can be made an attractive apex should be brought into position to replace the preexisting apex.

Four...Primary Branch: The first lower branch needs to be thick and full in the lower portion, and get smaller and thinner towards the top. Branches should be reaching out in all directions with plenty of secondary branches for developing the new bonsai structure.

Five...Secondary Branches and More: As you look at the branches you will notice many different sets and subsets of branches. The secondary branch should have plenty of foliage growing along it starting from the base. When selecting a conifer, choose a tree that has compact foliate and ideally short needles. If you are looking at a deciduous tree with actual leaves growing on it, choose one that has good prospects for change during the season with their unique berries, fruits, flowers, etc which change colors in the spring or autumn. Also keep an eye out for a tree that has developed a fine twig structure, which can be particularly attractive during the wintertime when you get to see the tree from a new, bare perspective.

When looking to style your bonsai there are some basic styles that we will cover. However, the main style that all beginners should start with is the straight trunk style called "CHOKKAN".

The training position is also critical in creating amazing bonsai. Ensure the bonsai is trained so that the middle of the tree is at eye level. Never look up at the tree from a sitting position nor look down on it from a standing position when working on your bonsai as this will create a distorted perspective and warp the overall styling of the finished product.

Introduction to Bonsai Styles

"Don't try and put seven western states in a pot"

— **Japanese bonsai lecturer**

THE STYLES

Formal Upright (CHOKKAN):

Slanting:

Cascade:

Informal Upright:

Raft:

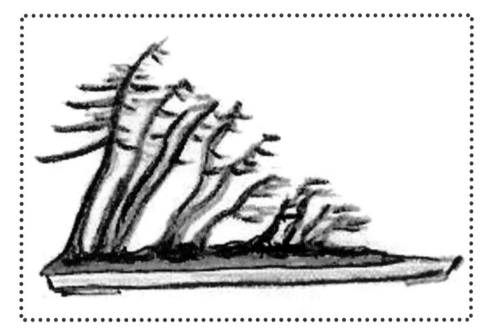

Literati:

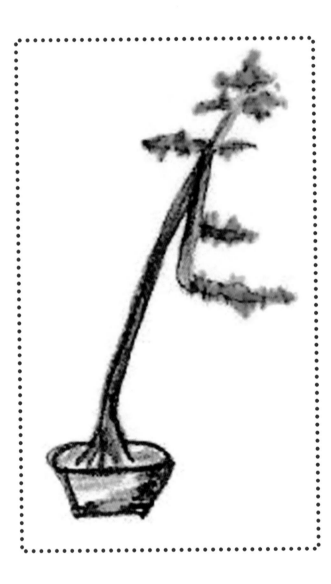

Windswept:

Broom:

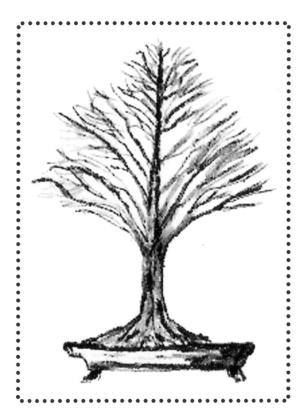

Twin Trunk:

Forest – Grove – Group Planting:

Clump:

STYLING 101: STYLING WITH "CHOKKAN"

"CHOKKAN", Japanese for "formal upright" is the basic principle style of all bonsai. When you finally get the chance to work with some quality tree material, you will now know what to do with it.

If you understand this style first, you will understand almost everything.

Imagine the shape of the basic formal upright or "CHOKKAN". You can bend it and do just about anything with the formal upright style, because the principles of the other styles are the same.

To use the principles of another style, you just have to view other material as formal upright with a bent trunk. Literally, you can bend the shape of the formal upright to informal upright, slant, windswept, cascade, and all kinds of cool styles.

You can do just about anything with the formal upright style.

Now, the whole principle behind the formal upright style is that the trunk is straight, which is to say, that if you tied a plumb line to the top of an informal upright, it would hang down directly to the NEBARI, "roots" in Japanese.

The informal upright style is when the trunk wanders in all sorts of directions, but the apex still lines up with the NEBARI.

If you know CHOKAN well, and grasp it well, you will understand the other styles as well.

Here is a great example of the formal upright

THE AURA OF BONSAI: CREATING BONSAI THAT BECKON

Now, something true of all bonsai style is that you want the tree to be slightly leaning toward you, in kind of a warm welcoming manner.

The first branch typically comes out a little bit forward, giving you that welcoming sort of look, as though that tree is trying to pull you into its aura. If you can really get that sense that that tree is beckoning you, then that tree will be able to take on a life of its own, pulling the eye and self into its composition. When people look at your tree they should get that sense of being drawn in instead of being pushed away.

Bonsai are always leaning towards you in a friendly kind of way.
This means you don't want anything sticking out in your eye, some
root sticking straight forward at you, if you can avoid it. You'd
rather have something more like roots that go out to the side as
part of your NEBARI.

THE FIBONACCI LAW OF THIRDS: 3 - 3 - 3

Ever heard of the Fibonacci sequence? Everything is in three. This sequence is also commonly seen in bonsai for balance.

Let's say I have a piece of quality material that has crappy material with little I can use down low. I go back to the Fibonacci sequence and go up the tree.

I am able to decide where the bottom branches start, as long as I'm thinking in thirds. First, I split the tree up into three equal parts and move up the trunk, grouping it into three parts. I look in the first third to find my first branch. If I happen to be working with a tree that has been in a forest situation I go to the second third of branches.

Oftentimes people tend to bend the branches like a bow, but instead you want the branches to taper sharply down. Why do branches come down? Because in nature older heavier tree branches hang down low, and you should attempt to model this same characteristic when training your bonsai branches in a downward manner.

And remember you're dealing in three dimensions too, so you can curve the branch in different ways, back and forth, plus up and down. Not so damn straight, please.

CREATING DISTINGUISHED CLOUDS OF FOLIAGE

Each branch is basically a tree form of its own. There are trees and trees and more trees! When styling, the idea is to create clouds of foliage floating in front of the hard trunk. This look is the look you're really trying to achieve and this is how you will get beautiful, great looking bonsai. But you must always be thinking, "This branch is a tree".

A STEP-BY-STEP BONSAI STYLING OVERVIEW

The first step to styling any bonsai is preparing the trunk and branches so you know what you're working with. Clean off the garbage and junk on the trunk, the dead bark, moss, sticks and other growth.

The first branch is almost always your longest branch. The longest branch can be on the right or left, wherever your good branch is.

The back branch gives depth to the tree's composition. Let's say you didn't have a back branch, sometimes you can fuzz that out in back to try and get some element behind it.

Next, your third longest branch... and in between this you want a front branch, to give it depth, and start blocking some of the straightness. You want a front branch somewhere in the composition, pretty low, if you can. You don't want your tree to be stiff and monotonous, looking like it grew up in an envelope.

If you have shorter branches, it gives the effect of age and thicker trunk and branches. And remember, every bonsai tree has an apex, sometimes it's more rounded, and you should be able to see it right away.

Sometimes your material just falls together right away. But often times it's the flaws that really make it interesting. This is key to awesome bonsai. You're balancing strength and grace all the time. Sometimes, strength needs chunkiness and fatness and muscularity of the trunk. There is nothing like a big beefy, powerful trunk to start out with to jumpstart your bonsai. This is another reason to collect trees from the wild. But, if you don't have the obvious presence of strength in your bonsai you have to see how you can put some grace into it.

Often times, when you're working on your tree, you should be aiming for an old, beat up looking tree with lots of character and that "ooooo-ahhh" factor. This emphasizes that natures has done something to it. When styling, keep this in the back of your mind always.

When looking at trees in the wild, they reach up high to where the light and air are prevalent. On the same note you should model your tree to be reaching after the light. Looking down at your tree,

its branches should come out in all directions, reaching into the light.

When looking down at the branches, front branches, back branches, side branches, theoretically you should be able to see all the branches. This is how trees grow in nature. Repeat after me, "Symmetry is bad. Balance is good."

That means you need to take advantage of negative spaces, and as Naka said, "Don't have those huge wads of foliage, instead leave room for the birds and bees. Trees need air to circulate through their branches."

THE MORAL OF THE STYLING STORY

Everyone one of us has to make up our mind which route we're going with depending on the tree material. Always do more with less.

To be able to look at that tree and say, "Damn, that's good" is what you want. That's the goal. The really great bonsai create their own reality with their own little sphere around them. Just like magical geisha dolls, bonsai should pull you into their aura; you are instantly transported up to that mountainside, or down into that valley, and if you can go there . . . that's good. That is true bonsai. That's where you want to go.

Choosing the Perfect Pot: How to Bring Out the Best in Your Tree

This often-overlooked part of bonsai is tremendously important in creating great looking bonsai. Choose wisely. The idea being that the pot suggests a unique perspective and landscape to harmonize with the tree.

Some common colors used for bonsai pots by bonsai masters include dark brown, gray, black, dark red, and dark blue which all symbolize nature, rocks, and other earthly elements.

The process for selecting a suitable bonsai pot is very important as the pot accentuates the tree's qualities and helps to create the right perspective. Remember to always select the pot for the already trained tree so you have an idea for what pot will look best with the tree's features. The pot should be selected after the tree has been styled and trained in order to better match the aura of the bonsai.

WARNING: Never, ever transplant your bonsai into a new pot and then begin to style and shape the tree. Rather, after shaping it can be planted directly into the chosen bonsai pot or in a temporary training pot with great bonsai soil.

During the transplanting into the new pot it may be necessary to cut the roots accordingly to fit the new pot. More than likely you will encounter some vertical growing shoots that should either be cut back or bent to better fit the pot.. Additionally, straighten or cut back any other roots growing sharply toward the base of the trunk.

The goal is to create a root system in the shape of an upside-down bowl. This root form can also be achieved when the tree is in a deeper training pot and the root ball is placed over a smaller pot or container, allowing for the roots to grow over and cover leaving a desirable root structure for the next transplant.

Place the tree into the pot and align the tree into proportion. A good rule of thumb is that the pot should measure approximately 2/3 the height of the tree.

If the height of the tree is much shorter and the tree is wide on the sides, you can determine the length of the pot by measuring the spread of the tree instead. Again seeing that it is about 2/3 the width of the spread. Never match the length of the pot to the width or height of your bonsai.

The goal is to harmonize the trunk size with the depth of the pot, with exception to cascading styles and multiple trunk styles. If you have collected the tree from nature there will be some more careful considerations to make and there is the challenge of working with the longer taproots.

Make sure the width of the pot should be only slightly narrower than the spread of the longest branches on both sides of the trunk. Normally the potter has already determined the length.

It is important that the style of the tree be somehow reflected in the pot, in the sense that the shape of the pot should harmonize with the style or character of the tree. A rectangular pot will better balance a straight trunk.

On the same note, a rounded pot will best compliment a curved trunk with softer lines. For curved trunks other pots can also work well such as oval, round, rounder-cornered, or rectangular pots even work nicely.

A powerful, twisted, gnarly tree should indeed reflect this through a similar looking pot to maximize the effect.

For cascading style bonsai that creeps over the edge and mimics a waterfall, the pot should harmonize and be deep and tall. Depending on the tree character, a pot that is more medium depth can also work quite nicely. Overall, the idea with a cascade style is that you never plant the tree in a shallow pot. On this style tree where the foliage cascades over the side of the pot remember that the length of the tree from the highest apex, right down to the very lowest branch, and the pot height, should never be identical. In some cases it has been known for bonsai masters in Japan to hang the tip below the pot using a display table or bonsai stand.

On the other hand, a more long shallow pot is more suitable for double trunk trees, twin trees, and other group planting styles. Remember to select a pot length that is approximately one-third or less than the height of the tallest tree. It is also common to plant trees of this style in longer more exaggerated pots to reflect a picture of a forest meadow or a large piece of land. This also helps to create the perspective that the trees are older and more mature than in reality, all while capturing a beautiful scene found in nature.

If you happen to find a nice chunk of rock and decide to create a root over rock type style bonsai, you will need a long shallow dish to place the rock planting into a solid foundation. Just be sure that the rock and tray or pot harmonize well both in color and size to compliment the natural character of the rock.

Glazed pots are good for most deciduous trees or broad-leaf evergreens. Select the color to harmonize with the color of the flowers, fruits, berries, seeds, and leaves of the tree. For example a flowering azalea would be complimented well by a pastel colored pot during the spring whereas a tree like a maple would look splendid with a dark colored pot to accentuate the bright red leaves in fall. Furthermore, an antique glazed pot can be used for both deciduous and conifer specimens and many people even use handmade bonsai pots that are both rare and expensive.

Unglazed pots work best with deciduous bonsai trees.

Best Bonsai Soils:
Ninja Tips

In response to a rapidly diminishing number of requests, we will, in fact, meet for the Bombastic Bastard Class focused solely on soil. Yes, dirt! This meeting will mostly be spent on what you want to do this year in preparing your soil and pots, and additionally going back to styling ideas and material, since we have done the wiring and styling stuff pretty heavily in recent chapters. Just looking at a few photos that bonsai newbies are sending in on the blog, made me realize that you guys are catching on pretty damn quickly. What we need to do now, I think, is to actually force you scum to work on raw stock without me snatching it out of your clammy hands — one of my favorite bonsai techniques.

I also need to renew my commitment to the whole art once again — last winter made me wonder if scrapbooking might not be a better activity for a person of my rough talents — I need you to help me push this weird cart back onto the highroad, and get it rolling again.

Let's make some dirt.

What do all great bonsai trees have in common? Amazing soil. The best bonsai are planted in soil that drains freely yet retains moisture. For free passage of air and water to the roots an ideal mix contains drainage materials, minerals like gravel or sand are great, but this alone may drain too quickly. Organic material is than added to balance out the mix as it lodges between particles, absorbing water and holding it for use by plant roots. In addition as the organic material breaks down it provides vital nutrients to the soil.

The truth is that you can buy potting mix sold specifically for bonsai, however it's quite easy to mix your own. Many bonsai hobbyists mix almost equal parts of a packaged planting mix, river sand, and sifted pine bark. Others use clay and other particles. Other great materials suitable for bonsai are akadama (clay pumice from Japan), black lava, pumice, decomposed granite, red lava, large river sand, perlite, coarse landscape planting mix, fine fir bark or orchid bark. These all contribute to good drainage with some organic matter.

The right mix is critical to the health and survival of your little tree. Overall the makeup of the soil should be clean, healthy and most importantly have excellent drainage. The stuff you buy at the local garden center is NOT always the best even if they claim it is bonsai soil. Much of the time this soil has too much peat and organic material, which is something to avoid.

You are seeking a soil that can maintain decent moisture but more important something that drains quickly and does not remain soggy for hours or days after watering; this leads to root rot and other wretched problems we don't even begin to discuss. Do not compact the soil too much and use too many larger particles like pebble, lava rock, or akadama, this may cause troublesome air pockets from not packing the soil enough either.

Once a tree has begun to take shape after wiring and bending, the new soil mixture should boost new growth and your tree will only grow faster and thrive. A good rule of thumb is to almost fully replace the soil mixture about 3-5 years after the first bonsai shaping to maintain the health of the tree. Now, this varies from tree to tree but just keep notes on your tree and remember to check every couple years or so to determine if the tree indeed needs this.

BASIC BONSAI SOIL NINJA TIPS

The best practice is to mix the soil according to the bonsai's need. Use coarser sand and small rocks for rapid growth of roots, especially for an unhealthy tree that needs to recover. The reason for doing so is that the sand and coarser material promote much better drainage and somehow stimulate better growth cycles beneath the surface to help your tree regain strength.

Use a finer mix when rapid growth is not as necessary and avoid using too much mulch.

Deciduous trees and other broad leaf evergreens require more soil and mulch with sand for optimum growth results.

Conifers need a lot more sand and less organic material like peat, soil, mulch, etc. because drainage needs to be improved.

BONSAI SOIL NINJA TACTICS

Collect soil from local mountains or growing sites with permission; be sure that there are other healthy trees, weeds and plants growing nearby, say for example along a stream or empty lot.

Many bonsai specialty stores online or locally supply a ready to use bonsai soil mix of pumice, lava, bark, and compost. It can be used for indoor and outdoor bonsai. Many enthusiasts use this bonsai soil as is, while others mix it with more pumice or lava. Everyone has unique growing conditions and develop unique soil mixes. If you have a local bonsai club to join they are a great source of local bonsai soil information to see what's working best in your hometown.

Many bonsai superstores also import high quality Japanese akadama, kanuma, kiryu, hyuga, all used in soil mixes for bonsai trees. Yes you can order them and make up some great mixes, but keep it simple.

Many times you can save a lot of money by getting pumice and lava from local sources. Money saved from hefty shipping costs goes directly back in your pocket.

Ensure your rocks and soil additives are graded and cleaned. These are great quality soil additives, free of insects or bacteria.

A particular mix you will hear a lot of bonsai enthusiasts speak of in the inner sanctum is the infamous Boons' Mix, described by many as being the best mix they have ever used for their bonsai tree collections. It consists of equal parts akadama, lava, pumice, a small amount of granite and charcoal. If you have never seen roots grown in this mix compared to most bagged soil mixes that you purchase at garden centers you would be amazed. Seriously, check this out.

Using the tips and tactics above, along with a little time and effort, you will come up with the perfect bonsai soil for your tree.

HOMEMADE MR. MIYAGI BONSAI MIX

Ingredients for Organic Fertilizer Mix - 5 lbs each of the following:

- · Fishmeal
- · blood meal
- · cottonseed meal
- · bone meal

Add mixture to 5 cubic feet of health organic material like composted topsoil from a hillside or local garden center

Add Sand

Add coarse materials such as lava rock, akadama, or larger pebbles

Boon's Mix (a great one to incorporate into your bonsai soil recipes that you can also find on mail order online or make your own)

Winterizing Your Bonsai

Okay Limp Limbs, did anyone but the most degenerately hardcore show up in the winter months for bonsai? Did you have any luck with your sleepy trees? Were you washed in the Blood of the Lamb? Probably not — I took one look at the ice and snow, and rolled back to my cardboard lean-to.

And, in that same vein, I think we will skip class this month. Our trees should be well asleep now, and I, for one, intend to join them whenever possible. By late January, however, we need to be thinking about how to handle another February freeze if necessary.

Until then, my brethren and sistren, may the coal in your mantle-hung stockings be turned into diamonds by your enormous asses pressing inexorably against the fireplace for warmth. I will cheerfully open all your sumptuous gifts in January, and I thank you for them preemptively.

Winterizing your bonsai is really fairly simple because during the dormant season your trees don't need as much water or light. Bring them into more sheltered conditions, out of snow and harsh, freezing temperatures. Some people even put their bonsai in a garage or shed during the winter months. Tropical bonsai, on the other hand, remain indoors and bypass this whole winterizing ordeal. Because your tropical trees won't go dormant, their care should remain almost identical year-round.

Wiring and Shaping For Perfect Balance and Harmony

All right, Renegade Arborists! Get good at wiring and you will have great looking bonsai. We show no mercy!

1. **Get your WIRES straight.** The ultimate wire for bonsai is copper wire. This is because it is easy to handle and can easily be reused and recycled if it is heated. Often times hardware stores sell galvanized wire but this is a bad choice of wire because it is springy and difficult to handle, and even worse will destroy the branch. Aluminum wire exists but yet again this is not the ideal choice because it is rather shiny and detracts attention away from the tree. If you can find an aluminum wire that has an earth tone color this will probably work.

    Just like people, wires come in all shapes and sizes. Each size fits a different branch and purpose. The standard gauging of bonsai wire is: 4,6,8,10,12,14,16,18,20,22,24,26. Professional bonsai masters all commonly use these.

2. **Get your WIRING straight.** First off, be sure to select the right size wire or your tree will be doomed at the hands of a wiring massacre. If you use too strong of a gauge wire on a smaller branch it will indeed crack the bark and cause problems. The size of the wire should be about 1/3 of the branch or trunk.

    Next, to gauge the correct length of wire you'll need, measure the length of the branch or trunk to be wired and add another 1/3 to it before cutting. This is a good rule of thumb to follow.

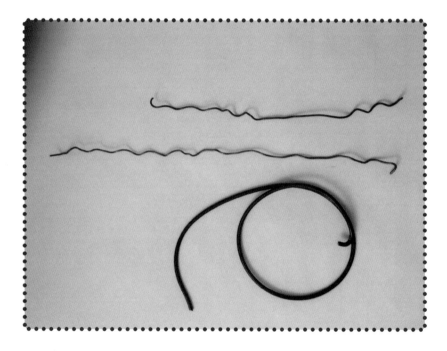

The best wiring starts from a strong foundation, the trunk. Always start from the trunk, and then continue wiring first the primary branches and then moving on to secondary branches and other smaller branches to better define the shape and perspective of the tree.

BONSAI WIRING PRO TIP:

Always wire towards the front, toward you. Yes, wire the branch in a motion towards you, not sideways or backwards. To put it another way, the best way to achieve this is by simply standing in front of the target branch and wire from the inside of the tree out, towards you, wire forward. This is also extremely beneficial to your tree by helping avoid crushing any leaves or small branches that might get underneath the wire.

Beginning at the trunk base, continue wiring each branch, using the appropriate size wire. Finish at the tip of the tree.

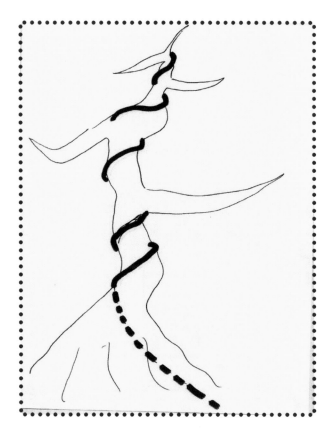

Start wiring from the rear of the tree by inserting the wire into the base of the soil about 2 inches, carefully avoiding any major roots. Ensure the wire is secured.

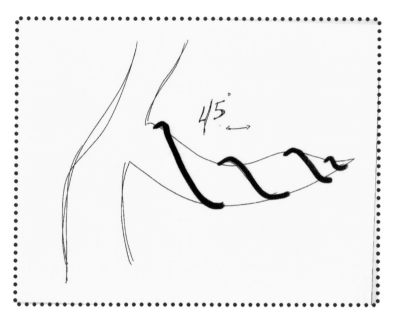

It is important to keep the angle of the wire approximately 45 degrees. This distributes the proper pressure to align the tree direction.

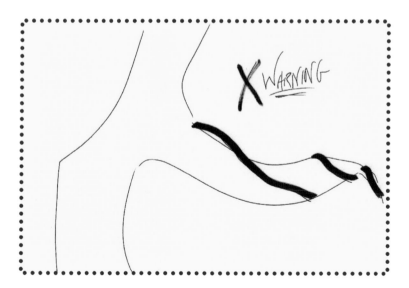

WARNING: Do not wire the branch too far apart

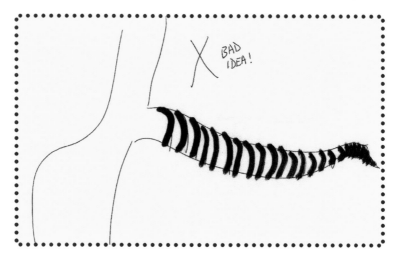

WARNING: Do not wire the branch too close together

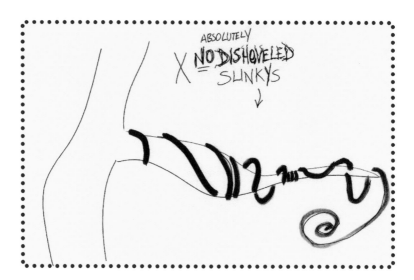

Don't get lazy either. If it looks like a disheveled slinky you may
want to start from the beginning again.

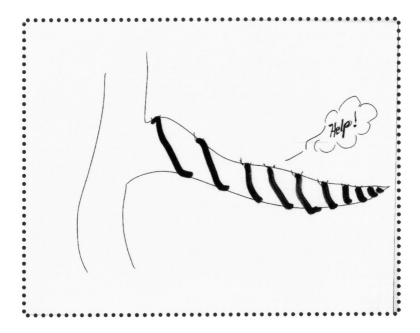

WARNING: Do not strangle the tree and make the wire too tight either.

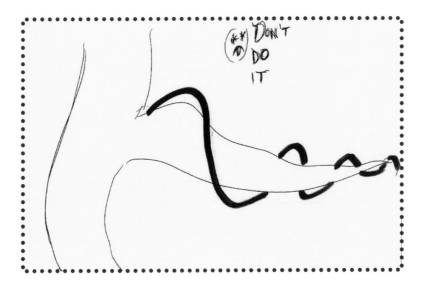

WARNING: You risk damaging the branch when bending if the wiring is too loose.

BONSAI WIRING PRO TIP:

Wind the wire in one direction only.

Right winding wire technique:

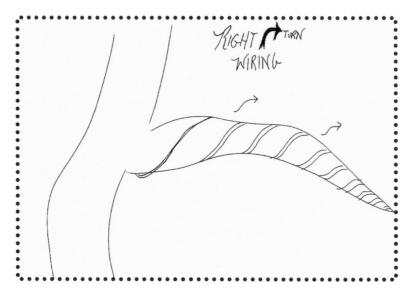

Left winding wire technique:

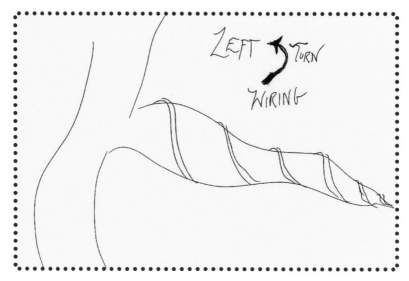

WARNING: Do not cross the wires.

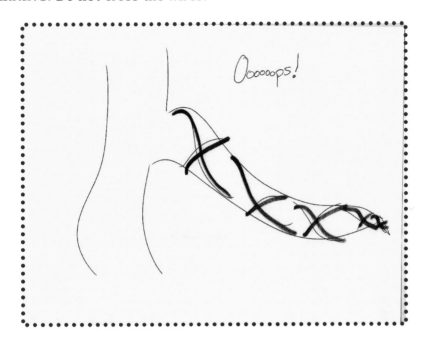

BONSAI WIRING PRO TIP:

If a larger wire is not immediately available, use several smaller wires, but wire one at a time and do not leave space between each wire. Ensure the wires are wired closely together for maximum leverage and strength.

Do not leave the extra wire extending off the branches. This could poke your eye out or get caught and rip off your branch. Simply cut it off.

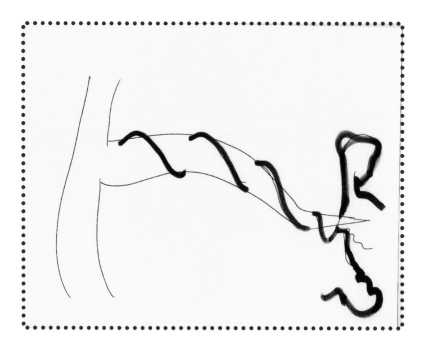

Do Not Wire the Leaves

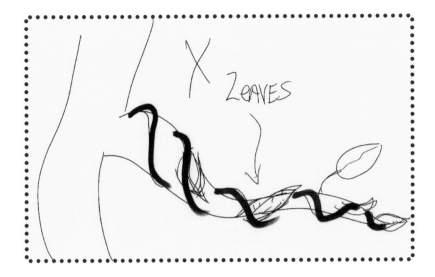

Do Not Wire Over Pine Needles

Do Not Wire Over Twigs and other smaller branches

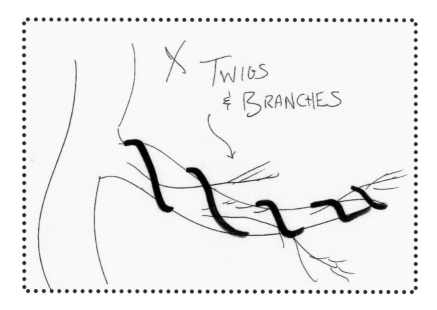

Do Not Attempt wiring multiple branches simultaneously

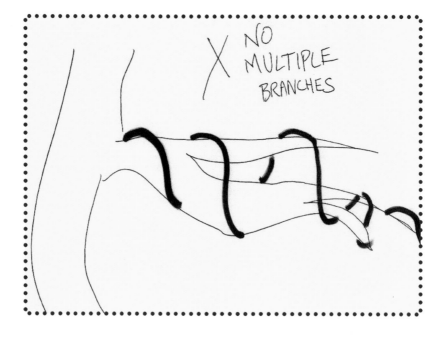

Do not anchor the wire on the branch as this is not secure and may cause unwanted scarring.

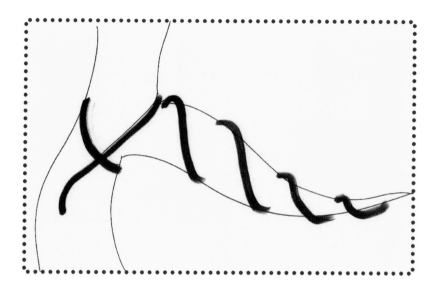

HOW TO PROPERLY WIRE YOUR BONSAI FOR MAXIMUM EFFECT

First, begin by anchoring your wire tightly at the base, and wind wire with quick sharp turns to secure onto the target branch.

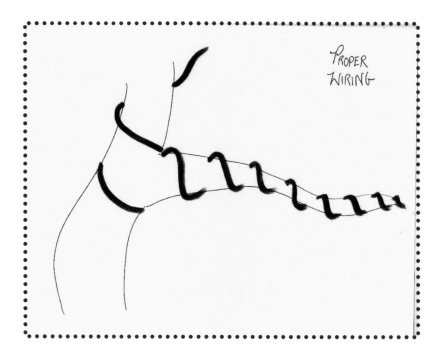

Do not do this carelessly or leave it loose at the base, as this will not properly hold the branch in position

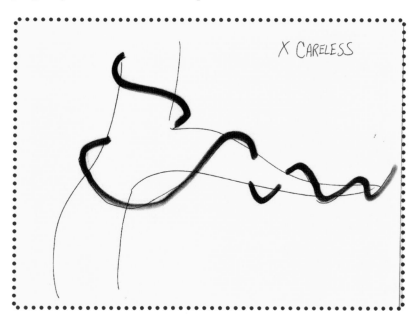

Do not start wiring from the base of the branches. You must ensure it is more secure.

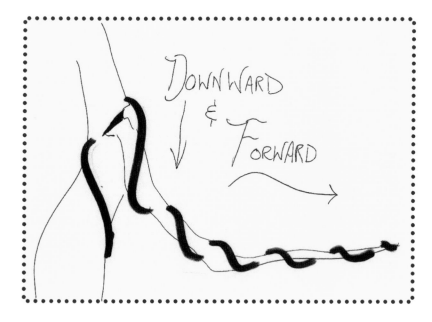

Wiring a branch downward is best accomplished by bringing the
wire over and then under

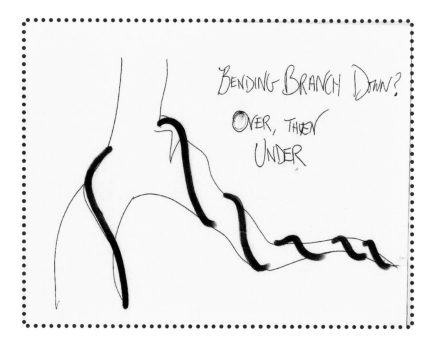

Do not bring the wire underneath the first branch as this creates
a weak spot and may cause the branch to snap when forced
downwards.

BONSAI WIRING PRO TIP:

For bonsai specimen that are very young or that have tender bark (white birch, crepe myrtle, and maple) be sure to wrap the wire with raffia or floral tape to help protect the bark. Do not wrap the branch; wrap the wire.

Furthermore for larger trunks that will not bend with one larger gauge wire, you can use two, or three or more wires, if necessary, until it will stay bent. Again use raffia or twine and this time you can actually wrap the bark and use a steel rod or several high gauge wires to bend into place.

MASTERING THE ART OF BENDING BRANCHES INTO PERFECT POSITION

Daniel:[after seeing Miyagi practice the crane technique] Could you teach me?

Miyagi: First learn stand, then learn fly. Nature rule, Daniel-san, not mine.
Daniel: Where'd you learn it from?
Miyagi: Father teach.
Daniel: You musta had some father, man.
Miyagi: Oh yes.

The ideal time to bend your tree into balance really depends on the season and you must be mindful of this. At different times of the growing and dormant seasons some trees are brittle and some are flexible. Timing this correctly is key to your success. In general, conifers like pines and junipers should be bent during the active season if possible. If it needs a massive bonsai makeover, do not bend in mid-summer because there is a chance that it will certainly loosen the bark, inner bark, and other internal things that will weaken or kill the tree entirely.

Deciduous trees are a bit different and the ideal time for bending is early spring before any sprouting occurs from the freshly growing buds. Another great window of opportunity for bending deciduous trees falls just before they go into dormancy in late fall. It is best to avoid bending after the tree has gone into dormancy with the cold weather as the tree sap is not flowing and branches tend to be brittle. However during the dormant months is an excellent time to study the branch structure that is normally hidden by the leaves during the main growing season.

Flowering plants should never be bent and stressed during the flowering period. Always wait until it finishes blooming to restore the trees strength and vigor.

BONSAI BENDING PRO TIP:

WARNING: Do not water the tree just before any major bending as this increases the likelihood of cracking and damage. The best rule of thumb is to hold the water for at least two or three days so that the plant becomes more flexible.

Avoid transplanting or loosening the root ball just before bending as this will overwhelm the tree and often result in bonsai death, and a new hobby.

IDEAL TECHNIQUE FOR BONSAI BENDING:

First, it is extremely important that you make sure the branch is correctly wired by following the instructions on wiring in this book. Once the wire is properly secured, begin to bend the area where the wire is wrapped over the branch by supporting the under part with the thumbs. Next, gently grab the branch while gracefully and firmly forcing the branch downwards. Avoid splitting the branch by simply keeping the thumbs beneath the underside.

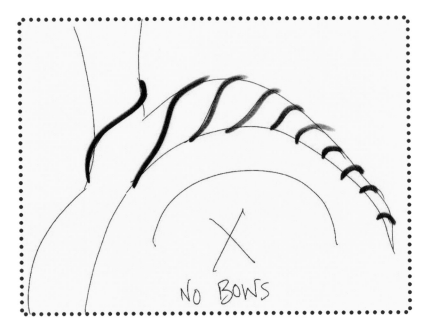

Avoid bending the branch into a bow shape

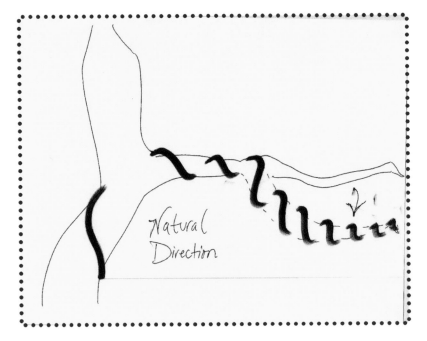

The goal is to bend the branch using the tree's natural direction

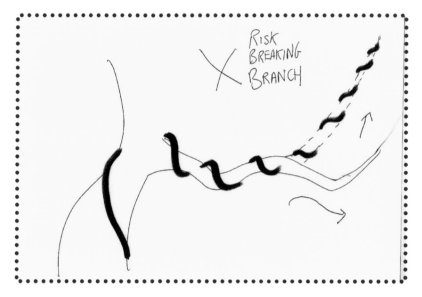

Avoid cracking the branch by bending against the original curve.

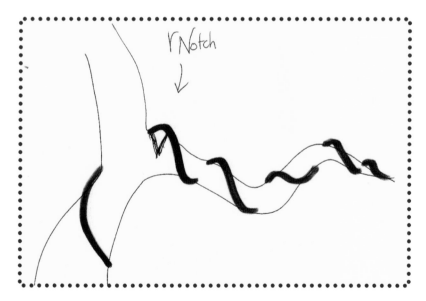

Target the first major bend close to the trunk and if necessary a small incision can be made at the top notch to help leverage the branch down into position.

Avoid making a sharp round bend right at the base of the branch

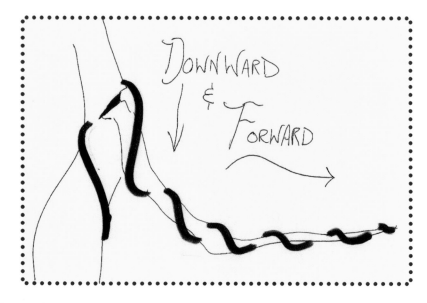

The goal is to align the branch naturally by bringing it slightly forward and downward.

BONSAI EMERGENCY – BROKEN BRANCH TRIAGE

Especially in the beginning of your journey in bonsai, you are likely to crack a few limbs. So in the case of this happening it is best that you have the right supplies on hand to quickly remedy the weakened branch. You can use a variety of natural products to cover over the gaping wound such as pinesap, egg white or even mud. The most common method is to use a commercial or bonsai specific tree seal to cover the wound. In addition, wrapping the area with floral tape or raffia with greatly aid in the healing process as the tree regains strength.

If the branch snaps and it is beyond repair, be sure to remove all fragments and chips of the split portion.

BONSAI PRO TIPS BEFORE AND AFTER WIRING YOUR TREE

1. Pre Wiring Tips

Be sure to first follow the correct directions in this book for how to properly wire. It is very important to only wire when your tree is in great condition. If indeed the tree shows any signs of weakness, such as weeping or yellowing foliage or anything abnormal, do not wire and train. If the tree was recently transported from another state or part of the world with a different climate, it is best to let the tree acclimate to the new environment. If this is the case, do not wire for at least a couple weeks, simply let is rest and get established before introducing any new stress. This will ensure your bonsai survives the wiring and you have a great looking bonsai that is alive and thriving.

2. Post Wiring Tips

Once the tree has been wired, treat is with extra care. Do not just leave it out in the elements with harsh sun, wind, rain, etc as this could quickly kill your new tree. Many people often make the mistake of trying to fertilize the tree right away, which can be extremely harmful and shock the tree. At best, avoid fertilizing your newly wired tree for at least two weeks even if it's during the growing season. However it is critical that you thoroughly soak the bonsai tree foliage, roots and soil right after the wiring process, especially if it wasn't watered before bending. Overhead sprinkling with a fine spray is also recommended.

IDEAL TIME TO REMOVE WIRE

The best way to know when to remove wire from you bonsai tree is by being observant and watching the tree closely. There is never a specific amount of time required before removing the wire as every tree is different and some grow slower or faster than others. Therefore, you must have a keen eye and consistently monitor the progress of the tree. If at any point you see the wire is cutting into the bark and inner bark, remove it at once. On average one can expect to have bonsai wire on for six months up to a year and even longer in some cases.

WARNING: Be careful to not damage the trunk or damage branches when removing wire. Do not use wire cutters and pliers in conjunction as this may easily snap a branch when a wire is being cut.

TWO STRATEGIES FOR WIRE REMOVAL

1. Unwind the wire slowly, without damaging other branches and bark. Do this in the direction it was originally wired.

2. Cut wire into small links of one to two inches, using your wire cutters to move down the branch or trunk.

If the wire has been left on too long and has already dug into the bark, carefully remove it so as not to peel off any bark and immediately apply tree seal to encourage quick healing.

Bonsai Fertilization

Daniel: *I don't know if I know enough karate.*
Miyagi: *Feeling correct.*
Daniel: *You sure know how to make a guy feel confident.*
Miyagi: *You trust the quality of what you know, not quantity.*

And the same goes for fertilizing bonsai. Although fertilizing forces new growth on your bonsai, don't over do it! And use high quality stuff.

Pruning: How To Reveal The Hidden Gems

Attention Tree Stumps!

Due to a series of bad breaks and misunderstandings, I'm late getting this on to you. We WILL march forward now that you are getting a better concept and we will concentrate on the beloved bonsai pruning which accompanies bonsai styling in creating the end result. I know we've done some of this before, but in no time at all you will know more than you probably wish to know about these pruning techniques to get your bonsai kicked into shape. I harp on it because if you know how to prune and create it, you will know the essence of all bonsai styling.

If you have some material, work it — practice on some random nursery stock, any style.

I'm sorry to be so late with this, but the dog ate my computer.

HOW TO EASILY PRUNE THE PRIMARY BRANCHES

Use a concave cutter as this is the best method and, because it provides a clean cut, the wound heals much faster and easier than a slow healing flat cut. Remember, leaving a protruding stubby knob is an eyesore and just looks bad, plus takes longer to heal. Don't do it.

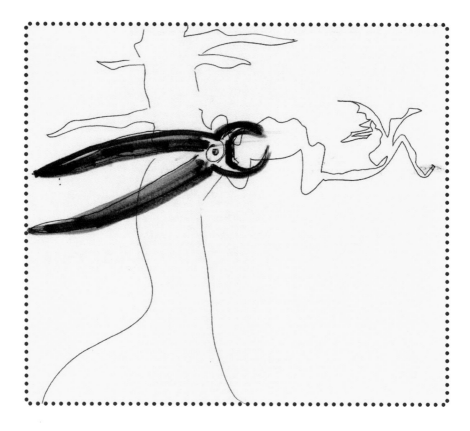

HOW TO EASILY PRUNE THE SECONDARY BRANCHES

Again, a concave cut is always the best way to go. The next best thing is to eliminate the branch with a flat cut. Finally, and yes I'm repeating myself, leaving a stubby knot is just plain wrong and should be avoided.

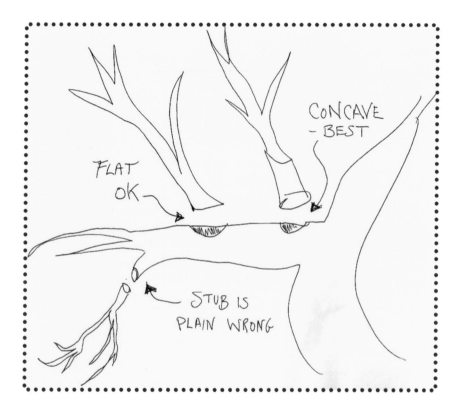

TRANSFORMING LONG UGLY BRANCHES

Many times when working with raw materials from the garden center or from the wild, it's often hard to find dense compact foliage. One way to encourage dense growth and more powerful branch structure is by using the following techniques.

1. Never cut the branch straight off because this takes extra energy and time for the tree to repair itself.

2. The goal is to cut off the branch diagonally with the cut wound facing upwards. Doing so will promote faster, easier healing.

3. Never cut with the cut wound facing downward as this is completely wrong and should be avoided.

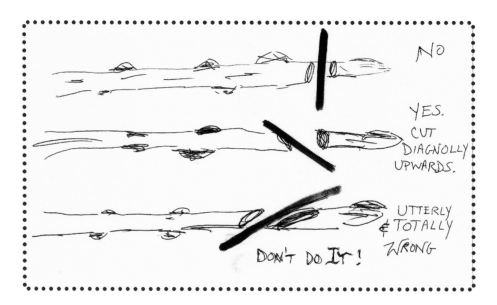

The correct method to use your concave trimmers is to angle it at the branch like it's about to take a bite out of it.

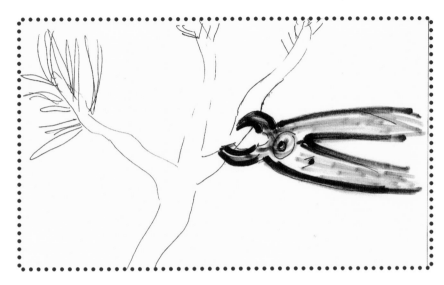

The incorrect method would be using the concave trimmers vertically, which will leave too long of a scar and look unsightly in the future.

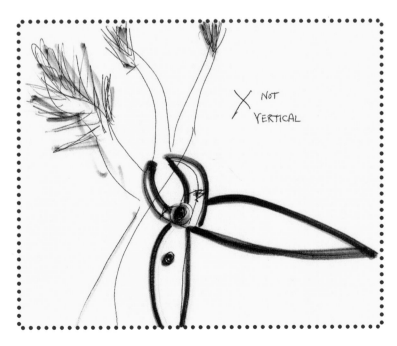

1. First, take hold of the branch that is to be eliminated

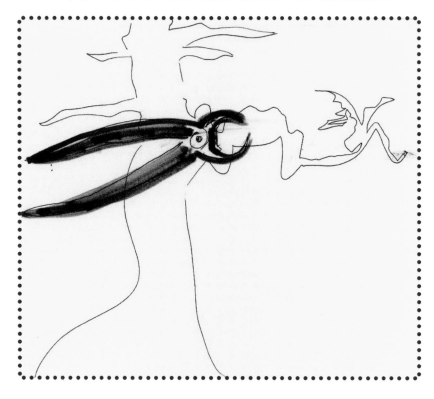

2. Make cut into bark with slight indentation in the bark to leave a concave hold. You can also turn the trimmer back and forth to cut into the bark for an extremely large branch or tree.

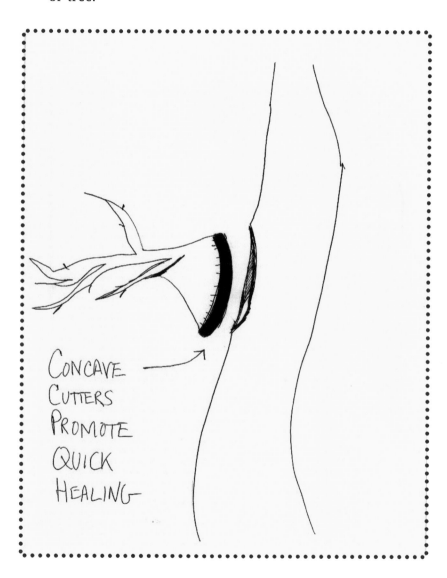

3. After the branch has been removed, carve off the scar of any rough spots and smooth down to look more natural and promote healing.

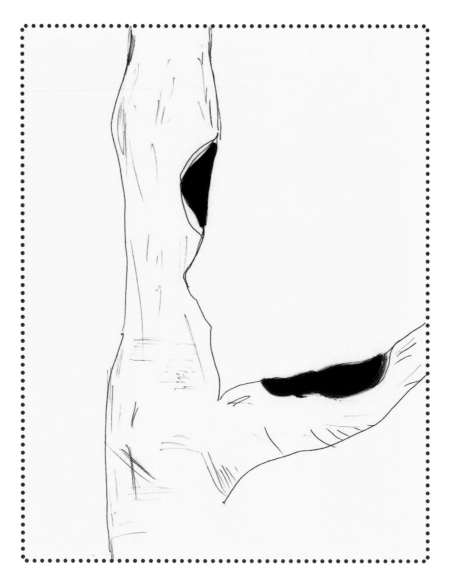

QUICKLY PRUNE ROOTS AND MAGICALLY DEVELOP STRONG BONSAI (ALMOST OVERNIGHT)

The life force of any bonsai is the roots, "NEBARI" in Japanese bonsai. A great looking set of roots underneath the soil and above the surface is a key task when creating any bonsai. Think of the roots as the mainframe of the tree. This is where the food and nutrients are mostly stored and where the tree gets most of its water. So naturally, it's extremely important to have a solid root mass so that your tree is extra healthy when you work on it and it becomes more and more of a bonsai. You never want to work on a tree that is weak and has not yet established a good healthy root system.

On bonsai that needs more density and compactness, cut back all strong shoots and leave the very short to sustain the tree. This technique will encourage more of the small fibrous roots to develop. When pruning the root system save the smaller roots by simply trimming just the very end of the points and not cutting back as hard as the longer, thicker roots.

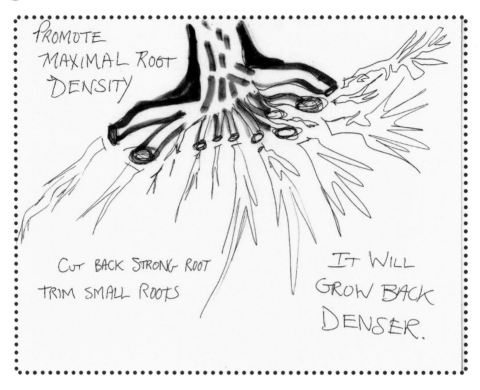

PROMOTE MAXIMAL ROOT DENSITY

CUT BACK STRONG ROOT
TRIM SMALL ROOTS

IT WILL GROW BACK DENSER.

To create maximum density and compactness, cut back strong, thick roots. Only slightly trim off the tips of the smaller roots to encourage more density.

UNDERGROUND BONSAI ROOT SECRET:

Here is a little known secret for bonsai tree that lacks good strong roots on one side. I have used this trick on my specimens of trees and it almost always works great.

1. Take a sharp knife or scalpel and inflict a series of small cuts in the place where roots are needed.

2. If you can get a hold of some rooting powder or vitamin B-1, now is the time to use it. Spread some of this over the area where you intend to encourage more roots.

3. Next, bury the tree in sand or in a pot of sand and within a few months roots will sprout. You may also want to consider using a greenhouse or placing a clear plastic trash bag over the potted tree to increase humidity levels, which helps while the tree buds new roots.

Wound the base of the trunk using a sharp knife where roots are needed + bury in sand + leave alone = magical new roots!

LEAF CUTTING PRO TIPS FOR DECIDUOUS TREES

Leaf cutting is used for most deciduous and broad leaf evergreens. It is not used for flowering, fruiting, berry trees or conifers. It is a seemingly brutal tactic that consists of removing certain leaves or even completely stripping a tree of its leaves artificially. This process mimics a second spring and forces new growth and leafing-out that results in many advantages.

A few major advantages with using this method:

1. Dramatically reduce the leaf size giving the impression of an older tree

2. Restores the leaf so that it will show to be more clear and robust in its fall color

3. Forces new smaller branches and increase dense, compact growth.

4. This will prevent any shock if transplanting is necessary during the growing season.

BEST TIME OF THE YEAR FOR LEAF PRUNING

This technique should be done from June to the early part of August in the northern hemisphere. It's dangerous to do this much earlier because the renewed leaf will actually get larger than the original and will not stay green until autumn.

On the other hand, if you get lazy and wait to long it will fail to re-sprout.

WARNING: Never, Never, Never, Ever use this method if the tree is weak and in an unhealthy condition or stressed. A weak tree or a very old tree may fail to re-sprout and eventually die.

When using this method be sure you do not leave any part of the leaf, small or big, on the tip or outer bark of the tree. If you leave any leaves on the tree, the energy will go to them instead of producing a new set of leaves.

After leaf cutting place the tree in a cool shady place out of direct sunlight for about a month while the tree recovers and forces next years growth. Never fertilize right before or right after cutting back the leaves as this often times will shock the tree into oblivion. Also be extra cautious not to over water during this time as the tree does not dry out as quickly as it does under normal conditions.

CORRECT LEAF REMOVAL

INCORRECT LEAF REMOVAL

NEEDLE CUTTING PRO TIPS FOR PINES, JUNIPERS, AND BEYOND

Just as deciduous leafy trees have a specific method for pruning, the same goes for pines, junipers and other trees. Normally you will implement this method on raw material or young trees. It's not a good idea to do this on bonsai trees that have been trained for more than 7-10 years, as the tree is older and more sensitive to aggressive pruning.

Examine your bonsai material and notice to see of there is long and bush, or long and curly foliage that needs to be removed. If so, cut back to about an inch long.

Some of the major advantages in using this technique are as follows:

1.   Encourages more dense, compact future growth by forcing the trees energy back inward

2.   Inner branches will now better develop new sprouts, as they will be exposed to more sunlight after the mass has been thinned out.

3.   Now you can wire and shape your bonsai easier than ever because you've cleared out all the junk and can see clearly now.

BEST TIME OF THE YEAR FOR NEEDLE PRUNING

The nice thing about pines and junipers is that you can prune any time of year, unless the needles are brand new and too tender to work with. In this case it should not be cut back unless you are completely removing the foliage down to the base to force other new growth.

JUNIPER SECRETS

Juniper, cypress and other scale foliage trees require a slightly different approach. It's a good practice on junipers to pinch back bushy foliage to avoid the tips browning from just using shears. Otherwise, if the foliage is extremely bushy and long, it may be sheared to reduce the length. Again if you use shears on these specimens the tip will turn brown but eventually will disappear.

WARNING: Do not cut back short needle conifers like spruce, fir, yew, cedar, etc.

On these trees the best method is to remove the dead or older needle growth further back from the tip of the new needles only if the tree is healthy. Be very careful as to not pull out the new needle growth. Only pull off the older needles after the new ones have grown out and matured. Another great way to do this is to simply cut the needles at the base so as not to damage the bark or break smaller branches.

Free Bonus: Get Amazing Bonsai Free (Nearly)

This is the number one secret to amassing a world-class bonsai collection. How do ninjas and bonsai masters quickly amass a collection of world-class bonsai in half the time it takes normal, everyday town folk?

We get out there in the great wilderness! And with proper permission, or what they call "wilding" permits, you can go harvest a tree too! Or, if the knees trouble you, get the nice neighbor kid down the street to do it for $20. Seriously this works, kids love digging up trees but you have to train them to be ninjas of course in order to return the trees alive.

THE TRIP: GETTING GREAT BONSAI FROM OUR LAST BONSAI CLUB DIG

I found this list from our last bonsai harvesting trip 2/29/12 - Enjoy!

Tools:

a.   Loopers or hand cutters/folding limb saw

b.   Shovel

c.   Hand trowel

d.   Pick/mattock

e.   Backpack

f.   Gloves

g.   Squirt bottle

h.   Permanent marker

Root Wrap etc:

a. Plastic or burlap

b. Strong string or wire

c. Bag of wet sphagnum moss

d. Water

At Car or Home:

a. Vitamin B or Superthrive

b. Pots, can, box

c. Basic soil- sand, pumice

d. Protected area, no wind, no sun, etc.

Personal Stuff:

a. Layers of clothing

b. Walking shoes

c. Hat, scarves, big handkerchiefs, bandanas

d. Water

e. Chapstick, sunscreen, toilet paper

f. Chair

g. Camera

h. Lunch

In The Field:

a. Find NEBARI- remove crap from around trunk

b. If trunk and roots are good, cut back excess growth

c. Start digging well outside. Rule of thumb-at least 4X girth wide and 3X girth deep minimum

d. Look for fibrous roots near trunk, mahogany colored

e. Cut large roots/tap or seal – keep ball intact

f. Create pedestal effect

g. Have wrap ready

h. Roll tree over, put folded plastic under ½, and roll back and unfold. Tie with lots of string, if bare rooted use wet sand or dirt.

Home:

a. Have pots & Bonsai soil ready

b. Put coarse gravel base-add sand-unwrap carefully

c. Water with vitamin B

d. Spray the top with water often

Until next time,

Happy Bonsai Hunting

What are you waiting for, get your hands dirty!

Joshua Rothman